This book belongs to _____

Color With Me!

Mommy & Me Coloring Book for Two

Autumn

Mary Lou Brown & Sandy Mahony

www.ingramcontent.com/pod-product-compliance
Lightning Source LLC
Chambersburg PA
CBHW081805280526
45789CB00008B/3002